Includes Five SAT Words to Know
MEETS STATE AND NATIONAL STANDARDS
Canada
The Maple Leaf Melting Pot Country!
IT'S YOUR WORLD
LIVE WORK PLAY LEARN
Where Do You Want to Go?
TIME ZONE • CULTURE • CUSTOMS • CLOTHING • HISTORY
Hey! It's Niagara Falls! Do you want to go?
FOOD • CULTURE • CUSTOMS • CLOTHING • HISTORY • LANDMARKS
By Carole Marsh

Live • Work • Play • Learn

GALLOPADE INTERNATIONAL

Gallopade International is introducing SAT words that kids need to know in our books. The SAT words in this book have a gray box around them. Students can look up the definitions and increase their vocabulary. Happy Learning!

Gallopade is proud to be a member and supporter of these educational organizations and associations:

Association for the Study of African American Life and History
National Alliance of Black School Educators
American Booksellers Association
American Library Association
International Reading Association
National Association for Gifted Children
The National School Supply and Equipment Association
The National Council for the Social Studies
Museum Store Association
Association of Partners for Public Lands
Association of Booksellers for Children

At the time of publication, all websites referenced in this document were valid. However, due to the changing nature of the Internet, some addresses may change or the content become less relevant.

It's Your World Books

Africa: A Safari Through Its Amazing Nations!

Australia: The Land Down Under for Mates of All Ages!

Canada: The Maple Leaf Melting Pot Country!

China: A Great Wall Runs Thru It!

Egypt: An Ancient Land of Lore; a Modern Land of Oil and More!

France: The Ooh-La-La Country Everyone Loves!

Germany: The Country of Fairytale Castles and Cutting Edge Science!

Greece: A Volcanic Land of Ancient Olympic Origins!

India: Land of Six Senses and Intriguing Mystery!

Italy: The Country of Amazing Fountains and Awesome Arts!

Japan: An Island Country of Endless Intrigue!

Mexico: A Colorful Land of Exotic Culture!

Middle East: Ancient Countries of Current Events Headlines!

Russia: The Great Bear and Its Dramatic History!

South America: A Continent of Countries of Amazing Proportions!

United Kingdom: The Country of Ships, Sealing Wax, Cabbages, and Kings!

Other Carole Marsh Related Titles:

America's Important Neighbors: Canada, Mexico, and Cuba

Table of Contents

A Letter from the Author

From the desk of CAROLE MARSH

Hey kids,

It's your world! It really, really is! Of course, you already know that, don't you? You surf the 'net, listen to satellite radio, watch television shows and movies set all around the globe–kids today are much more "worldly" than in the past, and that's a good thing!

Now's a great time to learn something about another country–such as Canada. Why? Because one day, you might actually visit there (if you have not already!). You might go to school there–many colleges have ties with international schools around the globe. You might even go on to work in a foreign country!

Many companies have positions in other countries. Companies are "going global" as fast as they can. They have branch offices, manufacturing plants, and customer service centers scattered around the globe!

So, ready or not: YOU are a Citizen of the World! And you'll want to be a good one. How do you do that? You'll find out everything you can about that country, how it's the same, and how it's different from your own country. What language is spoken there? What customs do the people observe? What foods do they enjoy? What do they do for fun? What has happened in this part of the world and what is happening there now? It's fun ... and the more you learn the more you will enjoy whatever global opportunity comes your way!

This book is a good place to start your learning journey–so take advantage of the world– IT'S YOUR WORLD, after all ... and guess what? It's a BIG world, after all!

Happy traveling and learning,

Carole Marsh
Always with passport in hand!

Why Should We Care About Canada?

Canada is located in the northern half of the North American continent. It is the second largest country in the world! Canada's 10 distinct provinces and three territories include bustling cities, rugged wilderness, and some of the most beautiful scenery in the world. Wouldn't you love to feel the wind in your hair as you ski down the powdery slopes of Whistler, or the Canadian Rocky Mountains? How could you resist the chance to witness the thundering roar of Niagara Falls?

From gigantic icebergs sparkling in the bays of Newfoundland and Labrador, to the old cobblestone streets of Montreal to the vibrant city of Toronto, Canada has something for everyone!

One day, you might visit Canada and see polar bears playing in the tundra of Manitoba, study agriculture at McGill University, view the Aurora Borealis from the Northwest Territories, or work for a Canadian company. It could happen!

Write home about it!
What will your postcard from Canada say?

Top Fast Canada Facts

Important facts to remember about the country of Canada:

- Even though Canada is the second largest country in land mass, it is only 34th in population, with 33 million residents.
- Canada was founded July 1, 1867, as a member of the British Colonies.
- Canada has two official languages, French and English.
- Ottawa is the national capital of Canada.
- Canada has the world's largest coastline on three different oceans—the Atlantic, Pacific, and Arctic.
- Canada is a democracy and has a prime minister and parliament.
- French explorer Jacques Cartier claimed the territory for France and named it Canada.
- The Canadian National Anthem is "O Canada."
- Canada's emblem is the maple leaf, which is on the flag.
- The Trans-Canada Highway is the world's longest national highway, with a length of 7,821 kilometers (4,680 miles).
- Canada has a national police force called the "Royal Canadian Mounted Police" or RCMP.

Jacques Cartier

Now, you figure out the rest!

1. This is the Canadian __ __ __ __.
2. The name __ __ __ __ __ __ comes from the Huron-Iroquois Indians and means Kanata, or "village."
3. Canada has __ __ __ time zones.
4. "From __ __ __ __ __ __ __ __" is Canada's motto.
5. __ __ __ __ __ __ __ cover almost half of Canada.
6. Aboriginals were the first __ __ __ __ __ __ to inhabit Canada.

Where in the World Is Canada?

- Canada is located in the northern half of North America.
- The United States is the only country that borders Canada.
- The Canadian Parliament is in the national capital of Ottawa.
- Canada's coastline borders three oceans—the Atlantic, the Pacific, and the Arctic.
- The Canadian city of Niagara Falls is in the province of Ontario.
- The highest point in Canada is Mount Logan in the Yukon Territory. Its highest elevation reaches 19,551 feet.
- Canada's 10 provinces are British Columbia, Alberta, Saskatchewan, Québec, Ontario, New Brunswick, Prince Edward Island, Nova Scotia, Newfoundland, and Labrador. Its three territories are the Yukon, Nunavut, and Northwest Territories.
- Canada has over 31,000 lakes. The largest one is Lake Superior, and is shared with the United States.
- Approximately 90 percent of Canada's population is concentrated within 200 miles of the United States.

Do You Know?

1. Canada was called "New France" in the 17th century and early settlers were called:
   a. The "Mounties" b. "les habitants" c. the New French d. Frenchadians

2. Canada borders which non-continental U.S. state?
   a. Massachusetts b. Oregon c. Alaska d. Florida

Look What I Found!

In 1497, explorer John Cabot began a long journey and sailed from England to the eastern coast of what is now known as Canada. He was captivated by its beauty and returned home with tales of bounty: fish in abundance and massive forests of tall trees. Word of Cabot's discovery spread quickly and encouraged explorers from other countries to also sail to the new land.

One of those explorers, French navigator Samuel de Champlain, sailed the new territory through the rapids of St. Louis above Montreal to New Brunswick and Nova Scotia. He returned to France and stressed the importance of forming a trade post along the St. Lawrence River. After he returned in 1608, Champlain decided on a place the Algonquin Indians called "Québec" and established a new settlement. Québec became a thriving trade center and the first permanent French settlement in the New World! The French called their new territory "New France."

Crosswords!

Use your new knowledge to fill in the crossword puzzle.

Across

1 The name Québec comes from the __________ Indians.

3 The French called their new territory __________ __________. (2 words)

4 French navigator Samuel de __________ founded Québec.

5 John __________ sailed to Canada in 1497.

Down

1 Cabot found fish in __________ and massive forests of tall trees.

2 Québec became the first ________ French settlement.

The Rich History of Canada!

There was a battle brewing! As word of the new, plentiful land in North America spread, both France and England staked claims for control. In the 1740s, the French became concerned about the British encroaching on the territory they had claimed, so they built a series of forts on lakes, rivers, and other strategic locations.

The British, looking to expand their empire, built their own forts in places including Halifax and Oswego. In 1750, British and French representatives met in Paris to try and solve these disputes, but were unable to come to an agreement. Battles continued and war (known as the French and Indian War) officially began in 1754. The war ended after the Treaty of Paris was signed in 1763. France agreed to give up control of the territory and New France fell under the rule of Great Britain.

French and Indian War

In 1931, Canada became a free and equal member of the British Commonwealth of Nations.

Today, Canada enjoys an open, free society. Its population is made up of people from different cultural, religious, and racial backgrounds. Its future looks bright!

Timeline!
Number these events in the order they took place, first to last.

___ Québec demands independence from Canada

___ The French become concerned about the British

___ Treaty of Paris is signed

___ The French and Indian War begins

___ French and British meet in Paris

Cool Canadians!

Matching!

Match these famous Canadian folks with their accomplishments:

1.________ I was born in Genoa, Italy, in 1450, but I am not known by my Italian name of Giovanni. I sailed from Bristol, England in 1497, and am credited with discovering Newfoundland, which is now a province in Canada.

2.________ An explorer and navigator, I mapped a large area of northeastern North America and have a lake in the United States named after me. I also started a settlement in Quebec, Ontario.

3.________ Known as "The Great One," I was born in 1961 in Brantford, Ontario. I hold the National Hockey League (NHL) career record for goals (885), and assists (1,190), and played in 17 NHL All-Star games. My number, 99, was retired by all teams in the NHL.

4.________ In 1979, while playing Scrabble with my partner Scott Abbott, I came up with the idea for the invention of a new board game called "Trivial Pursuit." Since it was released in 1982, over 80 million have been sold in 25 countries!

5.________ I was born in 1955 in Calgary, Alberta, Canada. I earned a doctorate in computer science from Carnegie Mellon University and am considered the "father" of the Java Programming Language.

6.________ After inventing the game "Basket Ball" in 1891, I received my medical degree, became the founder of the University of Kansas basketball program, and was inducted into the Canadian Basketball Hall of Fame.

A. Samuel de Champlain

B. Wayne Gretzky

C. John Cabot

D. Chris Haney

E. James Gosling

F. Dr. James Naismith

Guts and Glory Canadian Style!

A. Even though Canada was considered a safe haven for runaway slaves, she was kept in slavery by François Poulin de Francheville. In 1734, she was wrongly convicted and hanged for setting fire to Francheville's home, which then burned most of what is now known as Old Montreal. It is now believed she was innocent and was forced to admit her guilt.

B. This island in British Columbia was used as a leper colony for Chinese immigrants from 1894 until 1924.

C. Known as the "mystery man of Sandy Cove, Nova Scotia," he was found on the beach on September 8, 1863. There has been much speculation regarding how he arrived there, but his mystery was never solved!

D. This conflict was declared by United States President James Madison against Great Britain. Canadians fought alongside the British to prevent the United States from taking over Upper and Lower Canada.

E. This describes political efforts by this eastern province to secede from Canada and become its own country.

Mixed Up!
Match the paragraph to the word or phrase the paragraph describes.

DARCY ISLAND ____

____ **JEROME**

WAR OF 1812 ____

____ **MARIE-JOSEPH ANGELIQUE**

QUÉBEC SEPARATISM ____

With the Stroke of a Canadian Pen!

The writings of Lucy Maud Montgomery (1874-1942) were as popular with people of her time as the Harry Potter books are today! With her stories, Lucy made Prince Edward Island, Canada well known to people around the world who love to read. In 1897, she began submitting short stories to newspapers and magazines, and by 1907 she had published more than 100 works. In 1905, she wrote her first and most successful novel, *Anne of Green Gables.*

For a long time, Lucy wasn't sure anyone would ever read her novel. She sent her manuscript to several publishing companies, but was rejected each time. Frustrated and disappointed, she put the manuscript in a hat box and forgot about it. Lucy discovered it again in 1907 and decided to try once more to have it published. To her delight, the Page Company in Boston, Massachusetts agreed to publish *Anne of Green Gables* in 1908. It became one of the bestselling books in history!

The story takes place on rural Prince Edward Island, where Lucy was raised. The main character is an 11-year-old orphan girl named Anne Shirley. When siblings Marilla and Matthew Cuthbert decide to adopt an orphan boy to help on their farm, Anne shows up instead! The Cuthberts let Anne stay, and the rest of the book captures her life and adventures. *Anne of Green Gables* has sold over 50 million copies worldwide!

Anne of Green Gables

Write your own story!
Get out your pencil or pen. Write a brief fictional story based on where you were raised!

Uphold the Law!

RCMP

That's the motto of the Mounties, Canada's police force! The Royal Canadian Mounted Police (RCMP), or the Mounties, is unique in the world because this one group protects all of Canada's citizens from coast to coast. That's a lot of work!

The Mounties were originally known as the North-West Mounted Police (NWMP). When the force was founded in 1873, it was made up of just 300 men on horseback. Those men made sure that traders from the United States didn't unfairly trade cheap whiskey for buffalo hides, which were much more valuable.

By 1885, the force had grown to more than 1,000 men! Eleven years later, Canadian Prime Minister Sir Wilfrid Laurier decided to shrink the police force and then got rid the NWMP altogether. But without the NWMP, who would protect Canada's citizens? By 1919, the Canadian Parliament had realized the importance of the NWMP's service, and voted to combine the force with its eastern counterpart called the Dominion Police. The Royal Canadian Mounted Police were born!

Today, the 26,000 men and women of the RCMP help fight crime throughout Canada, and assist other police forces throughout the world. "We Always Get our Man" is often heard in movies and on television as the Mounties' motto, but it's not. The Mounties' real motto is "*Maintiens le droit*," which is French for "Uphold the law."

Word Play!
Use the words on the right to make as many words as you can with three letters or more.

Canadian Mounted Police

______________	______________
______________	______________
______________	______________
______________	______________
______________	______________
______________	______________
______________	______________
______________	______________
______________	______________
______________	______________
______________	______________

CN Tower, A Site to See!

What "towers" over the Toronto skyline? It's the **CN (Canadian National) Tower!** This communications and tourist tower stands just over 1,800 feet tall. Construction on the CN Tower began in 1973. The tower opened to the public in 1976. It is located on the north shore of Lake Ontario and has four viewing levels. 360 The Restaurant is located at 1,150 feet and rotates once every 72 minutes to give an unobstructed panoramic view of Toronto. Close to the top, at 1,465 feet, Sky Pod is the world's highest public observation deck. Each year, approximately 2 million people visit the CN Tower!

1,537 people worked five days a week, 24 hours a day to build the CN Tower.

A metal staircase reaches the main deck level after 1,776 steps, and the Sky Pod level after 2,579 steps; it is the tallest metal staircase on Earth.

The CN Tower dims unnecessary exterior lights during bird migration seasons to prevent bird injuries.

The tower changes the colors of its lights for holidays and major events.

The total weight of the tower is 130,000 tons.

Create your very own travel pamphlet. Concentrate on an area that interests you. Perhaps you enjoyed learning about the people. Or maybe it was the monuments that interested you. Fold a piece of paper into three sections. This will give you six areas on which to put information.

Left Is Right!

Customs and culture vary widely from country to country. Sometimes they vary in different regions of the same country. Here are customs and cultural differences observed by Canadians!

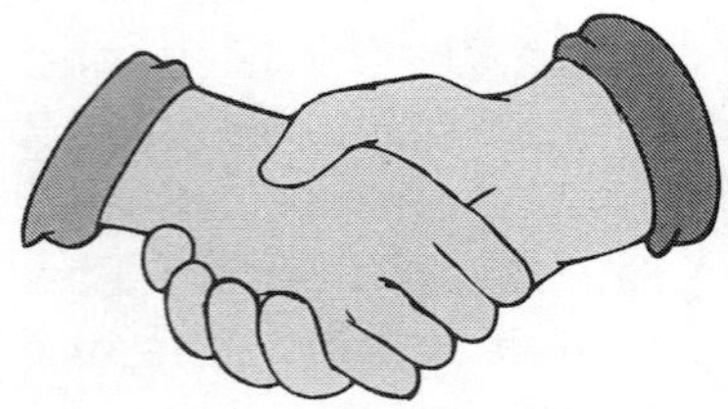

- The handshake is the most common greeting.
- French Canadian friends greet each other by lightly kissing once on the left cheek, then once on the right cheek.
- You should not use someone's first name until you are asked to do so.
- White lilies are associated with funerals, and should not be given as a gift.
- The fork is held in the left hand and the knife in the right. You hold them the opposite way in the U.S.!
- Tourtiore, a meat pie made from pork, potatoes and onions, is a popular Christmas Eve meal in many parts of French Canada.
- The Calgary Stampede is a huge festival and rodeo held in Calgary, Alberta every July. More than 1 million people attend!
- Before a couple weds in Manitoba, family and friends host a public dance called a social. The money raised from selling tickets to the dance is used toward the couple's new life together.

Create your own!
As we have seen, customs and cultural activities can help define who we are. Think about your family and friends and come up with some new customs for everyone to try.

What Do They Speak in Canada?

The official languages in Canada are French and Canadian English. They may speak English, but some of their words are different.

Match it up!
Below are some common Canadian English phrases or words. See if you can match them to the English word.

Canadian English	English
bunny hug	sneakers
fire hall	colored pencil
garburator	hoodie
parkade	napkin
pencil crayon	knitted hat
runners	fire station
serviette	bathroom
tuque	garbage disposal
washroom	parking garage

Happy Holidays!

Canadians have 10 national holidays. Some of them are just like our holidays, like New Year's Day, Labour Day, and Christmas.

They also have a holiday like our **Veteran's Day** celebrated on November 11th. They call it **Remembrance Day**. Canadians also have a **Thanksgiving Day,** but they celebrate it in October. Other holidays celebrated by Canadians are **Good Friday, Easter Monday, Victoria Day, Canada Day,** and **Boxing Day.**

Victoria Day is a celebration of Britain's Queen Victoria's birthday and the birthday of the current monarch. **Boxing Day** is always celebrated on December 26th, the day after Christmas.

Canada Day celebrates Canada's birthday. It is celebrated on July 1st every year. Canadians celebrate their nation's birthday much like we do—with fireworks, parades, and picnics!

Write it down!
Below, write a letter to a friend.
Describe a Canada Day celebration.

Canada on the Stage and in the Museums

Since Canada is such a beautiful country, Canadian artists reflect the vast landscape in their paintings. The country's arts culture also reflects its most valuable resource—the children! Canada is a pioneer of children's folk music and has a richly diverse culture of puppetry.

1.

3.

Notes

1. Puppets Up! is an international festival that celebrates the folk art of puppetry.

2. Four Seasons Center for the Performing Arts is home to the Canadian Opera Company.

3. *Bay of Islands* by Franklin Carmichael comes from the Group of Seven, a troop of landscape painters who founded the Canadian art movement.

4. The fiddle is the principal instrument in Canadian folk music.

5. *Anne of Green Gables*, by Lucy Maud Montgomery, has been translated into 15 languages and was made into a 1985 TV movie.

2.

5.

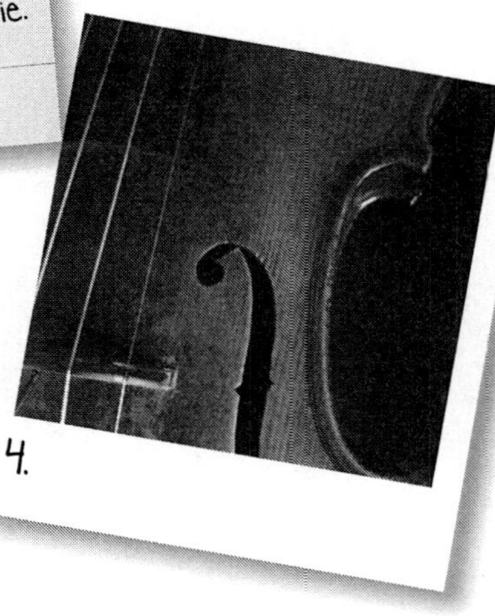

4.

What's for Dinner?

Traditional Canadian dishes vary by region. People on the coasts enjoy a lot of fish in their diets. Many of their dishes are just like ours, but some have a distinctive Canadian flavor! Take a look below and learn about some traditional Canadian dishes.

Clam chowder is a stew made of clams.

Fiddleheads are fern shoots that are lightly boiled and served with butter.

A tourtière is a meat pie made of pork that is served on Christmas Eve in Québec.

Maple syrup is considered the national food. It is poured over pancakes and even over snow!

Bon Appétit! (literally, good appetite. Enjoy!)

RECIPE

Always ask an adult for help when cooking!

Maple Ice Cream

INGREDIENTS

3/4 cup heavy cream
3 tablespoons maple syrup
1 cup light cream
2 teaspoons vanilla extract
4 tablespoons powdered sugar
1/2 cup whole or 2% milk
additional syrup to pour on ice cream

mmmmmm....this was good!

DIRECTIONS

1. Whisk heavy cream and maple syrup in a mixing bowl until stiff.
2. Gently heat light cream, vanilla extract, powdered sugar, and milk in a medium saucepan. Cook over low heat, stirring continuously until sugar is dissolved.
3. Stir the heavy cream and maple syrup mixture into the saucepan ingredients. Pour into a medium container and cover with a lid.
4. Freeze mixture for about 3 hours or until firm.
5. Scoop ice cream into bowls and pour on additional maple syrup as desired.

He Shoots, He Scores!

Canadians love their hockey! Hockey is called the fastest game on ice, and some of the best players can skate more than 30 miles per hour! Every year, 30 teams in the National Hockey League compete for hockey's most coveted trophy, the Stanley Cup. The trophy is named after Sir Frederick Arthur Stanley, who donated it in 1892. Each year, the name of every member of the winning team is engraved on the Cup. The Stanley Cup travels around the world on display. In 2007, it was brought to Afghanistan so the Canadian troops could see it. Talk about boosting morale!

Figure it out!

Figure out the answers to these questions about hockey.

Hockey Game

1. The NHL formed in 1926. The Montreal Canadians have won the Stanley Cup 23 times and the Toronto Maple Leafs are second, winning it 13 times. How many years have other NHL teams been awarded the cup?

___

2. After the Stanley Cup is awarded to the winning team, a summer celebration begins and each player and team staff member get to enjoy it for 24 hours. If there are 50 people with the winning team, how many hours will it take until everyone has their 24 hours?

___

Fast Fact:

The Montreal Canadiens hold the record for most consecutive championships with five (from 1956-1960).

Québec— The Centerpiece of New France!

Québec

If you ever visit Québec, you might want to learn a few French words first. Québec is a province (like a state) in Canada, but French is its official language! Québec is the largest province in Canada by area. It borders Ontario, New Brunswick, and Newfoundland.

During the 17th and 18th centuries, French settlers founded the colony of New France, which we now know as Canada. Québec became the wealthy capital of New France. Before 1763, this French North American Empire was a very large territory. It included the St. Lawrence River valley and the Great Lakes region, as well as the Missouri and Mississippi rivers. It also extended from the Ohio River valley all the way to the Gulf of Mexico!

In July of 1867, Québec was named one of the original four provinces of Canada, along with Ontario, New Brunswick, and Nova Scotia. Since that time, Canada has added six other provinces and three territories. On July 3, 2008, Québec celebrated the 400th anniversary of its founding by French Explorer Samuel de Champlain!

Word Fun!

Match the name of the historical landmark with the type of attraction it is.

Basilique Cathédrale Notre-Dame, Montmorency Falls, Cartier-Brèbeuf National Historic Site, National Battlefields Park

Church	Historical/Monument	Natural

Canada Did It First!

Cold and Fast!
Joseph-Armand Bombardier is the father of the snowmobile. He created his first prototype when he was only 15 years old.

Coffee Anyone?
James A. Gosling invented the Java computer programming language in 1991.

Clear the Path!
Canadian Arthur Sicard invented the first snow-blower in 1925.

Three Point Play!
Even though basketball is considered an American sport, its inventor, James Naismith, was born in Canada.

Word Fun!

This is fun to do with someone else. Ask a friend for words to substitute for the blanks in the story. Their word substitutions will have a humorous effect when the resulting story is then read aloud.

I want to be the first person to ______________ (ACTION VERB)

across ______________ (COUNTRY)! I've been training for this

since ______________ (MONTH). I'm in ______________ (ADJECTIVE) shape.

My ______________ (ADJECTIVE) adventure will begin on

______________ (FAVORITE HOLIDAY). I won't be hard to miss,

I'll be the one wearing a ______________ (COLOR)

______________ (ARTICLE OF CLOTHING) and a pair of matching

______________ (FOOTWEAR). My faithful friends

______________ (FAMOUS ATHLETE) and

______________ (CARTOON CHARACTER) will be there to cheer for me.

I'm bringing my ______________ (NOUN) along for good luck.

I'm confident I'll be the first!

What a Gas!
Abraham Gesner invented kerosene in 1846 and is considered the founder of the modern petroleum industry.

Helping on the Move!
Dr. George J. Klein invented the electric wheelchair, which has helped thousands of quadriplegic people get around.

Everybody Dance Now!
Canadian scientist and composer Hugh Le Caine invented the first music synthesizer.

Ride 'Em Cowboy!

Cowboys at the Rodeo

If you like bucking broncos, rides, and games, then Calgary, Canada is the place for you! Each July, Calgary is home to the Calgary Stampede, which is known as the Greatest Outdoor Show on Earth. The Stampede combines a rodeo, festival, and exhibition into one fun-filled event!

A former cowboy from Wyoming by the name of Guy Weadick organized the first Calgary Stampede in 1912. About 100,000 people came! Weadick also introduced many unique events, including chuck wagon racing, downtown celebrations, and community activities. These events helped the Stampede attract more and more people each year.

At the Stampede you can watch the world's best rodeo athletes compete in bull riding, bareback horse riding, and steer wrestling events. The winners might get more than $1 million in prize money! In addition to the rodeo, the Calgary Stampede holds livestock competitions and features theme areas like an Indian village or a blacksmith shop. Weadickville is the re-creation of a Calgary street from 1912!

Today, more than 1 million spectators attend the Calgary Stampede every year. It has become the largest event of its kind in the world!

Tell Me More!

Write five questions you have about the Calgary Stampede. With an adult, get on the Internet to try to find the answers to your questions.

Example: How many cowboys compete in the rodeo?

1. ______________________________?
2. ______________________________?
3. ______________________________?
4. ______________________________?
5. ______________________________?

Je t'aime Montreal!

If you want a flavor of what it's like to visit France you need only look north—to the city of Montreal, Québec, Canada! The cultural center of Québec, Montreal is the largest French-speaking city in North America and the second largest in the world behind Paris. As a matter of fact, the city's charter states that French is its official language. *C'est magnifique*!

Montreal will please anyone who loves beautiful buildings. Saint Louis Square has a variety of Victorian style homes. Many are owned by writers, actors and musicians. You never know when you may see a Canadian celebrity in the area!

Notre-Dame Basilica

Notre-Dame Basilica in Montreal is an amazing work of architecture. It was the first Gothic Revival style church built in North America. Building began in 1824, and took only 35 months to complete. When the church opened in 1829, Notre-Dame Basilica was the largest house of worship of any religious denomination in North America.

Revealing Answer!

Follow the instructions to reveal a common architectural feature of Victorian homes:

1. Cross off the first two letters
2. Cross off the fourth letter
3. Cross off any letter L
4. Cross off the 13th letter of the alphabet
5. Cross off the letter Q

X P T F L U R R M Q E L T

Lights, Camera, Action!

Did you know that one of the most important film festivals in the world is held in Toronto, Canada? The Toronto International Film Festival (TIFF) began in 1977 and has become one of the biggest on the planet! For 10 days every September, the TIFF shows 200 to 400 films from all over the world. Many films shown at this festival go on to win Hollywood awards!

For the last 10 years, the winners of the Academy Award for Best Foreign-Language Film were first shown in North America in Toronto. In 2007, most of the Oscar nominees for Best Picture premiered at the TIFF!

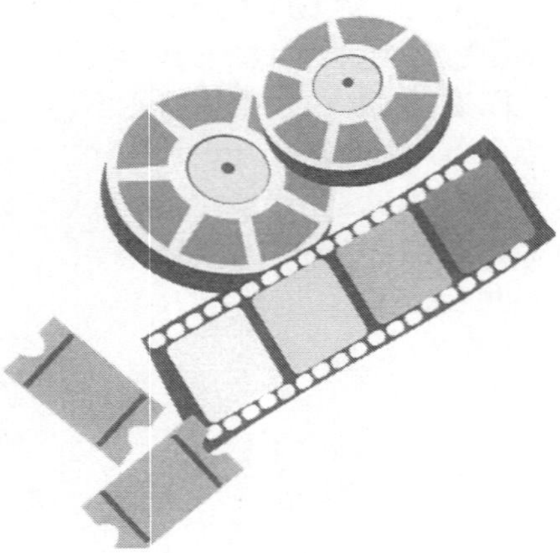

If you attend the festival, you will find most of the activities in the Yorkville neighborhood of Toronto. With more than 20 screens showing films, you should have no trouble finding something you like! Who knows, you may even bump into your favorite movie star!

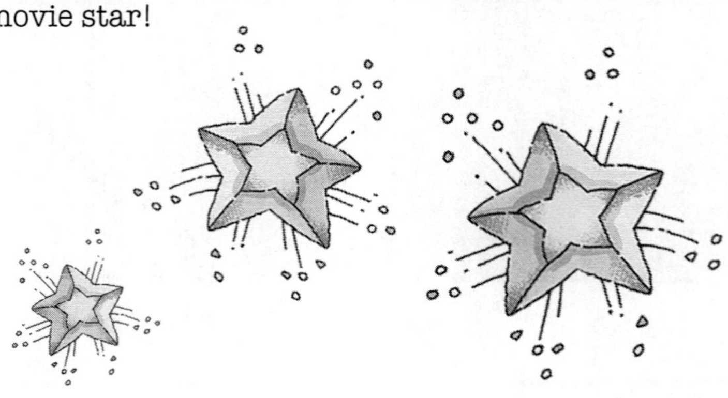

Cross it off!
Starting with the first letter, cross off every other letter to reveal the name of the neighborhood where the TIFF is centered.

A Y W O Q R P K J V Z I D L N L G E

____

Frozen Fish!

When you think of fun activities you can do on a frozen pond, does fishing come to mind? If you live in Canada it does! In Canada, ice fishing is a popular outdoor pastime during the winter months. Ice fishing might sound easy, but there is a lot to learn before you can safely and successfully reel in a whopper!

You may want to start by finding some professional help! Because ice fishing is so popular in Canada, there are many professional ice fishing guides who can help you learn how to do it correctly. Your guide can lead you to the best ice fishing locations in Canada. Depending on where you are, you might fish for lake trout, northern pike, walleye, whitefish, or rainbow trout.

Before you set out on your expedition, make sure you're dressed warmly! It's freezing out there! Once your guide locates the right spot, he or she will drill several holes in the ice using a tool called an auger. After the holes are drilled, you can lower your baited hook into the water and wait for the hungry fish to arrive!

Did you know that ice fishing is usually done in a house? Permanent or semi-permanent shacks are built over the ice or are hauled by trailer and gently placed on the ice to protect fishermen from the elements!

Figure it out!

Below, list six things you might want to bring when ice fishing in Canada.

1. ______________________ 4. ______________________

2. ______________________ 5. ______________________

3. ______________________ 6. ______________________

If the Shoe Fits!

What made you decide which shoes to wear today? Was it the style? Were you doing something athletic? Maybe you were going out to jump in puddles! Shoes tell a lot about a person, and Sonja Bata is an expert on the subject of shoes!

Bata has been traveling the world and collecting shoes since 1940. She helped to open the Bata Shoe Museum in Toronto, Canada in 1995. The museum displays more than 12,500 pairs of shoes and spans 4,500 years of history! There are even examples of 20th century celebrity shoes, including the Beatle boots that John Lennon wore and Marilyn Monroe's red leather pumps!

For the past 30 years, Bata's foundation has provided funding for research and travel to study the origin of shoes. These studies have been performed in Canada, Europe, Asia, Alaska, and Siberia. Maybe someone will want to study your shoes someday! If so, be sure to put your best foot forward!

Dress up!

Help Christina get dressed to travel through Canada. She has the shoes, but she needs an outfit! Choose which outfit she'll wear. Color the clothing, and draw a line from the piece of clothing to Christina or cut the clothing out and dress her up!

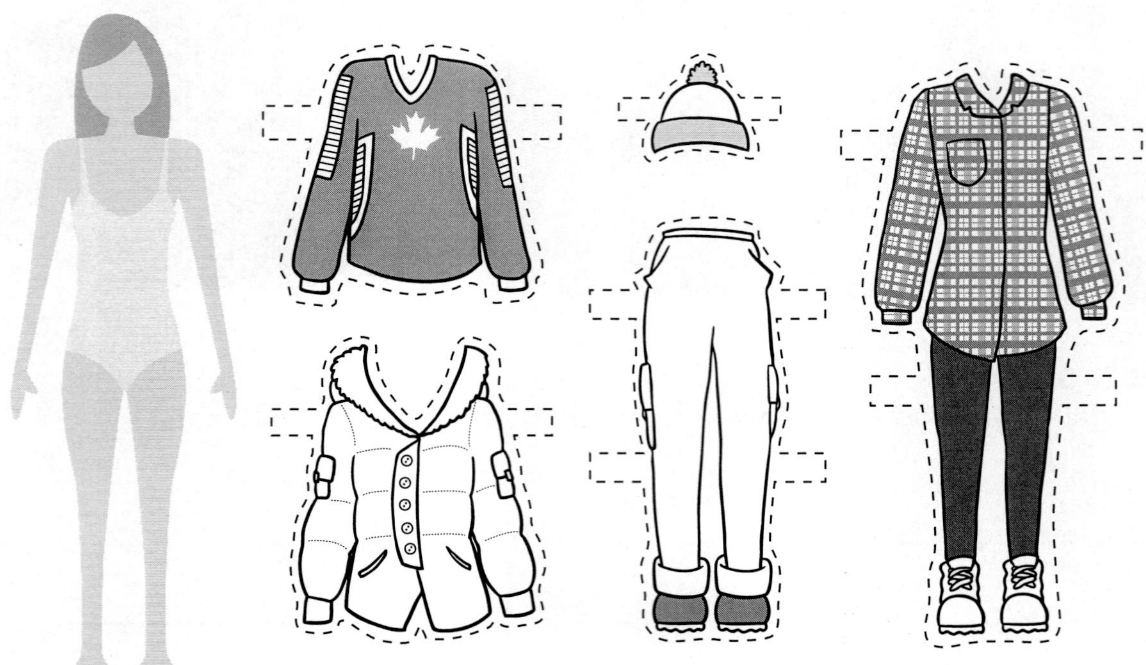

Assorted Architecture!

Figure it out!

Use the following clues to figure out this famous structure in Toronto, Canada.

- This building is home to Canada's largest English Catholic diocese.
- It was built from 1845 to 1848 by English architect William Thomas, with funding from Irish immigrants.
- The building was patterned after a style used in 14th-century gothic York Minster cathedral in England.
- The cornerstone of the building was laid on May 8, 1845 by Bishop Michael Power, the first Bishop of Toronto.
- The patron saint of this structure is Michael the Archangel.
- The building is located on Church Street in Toronto.

Canadian, English, or French?

Figure it out!
Both English and French are spoken in Canada. You know your English words, but here are a few French words you might use in Canada!

English Word	Original French Word
cathedral	*cathédrale*
museum	*musée*
river	*rivière*
history	*histoire*
explorer	*explorateur*
fisherman	*pécheur*
city	*ville*
church	*église*
visitor	*visiteur*
music	*musique*
boat	*bateau*
guardian	*tuteur*
brother	*frère*
architect	*architecte*
traveler	*voyageur*

____

____

____

____

Further Resources

U.S. Embassy in Canada
P.O. Box 866, Station B
Ottawa, Ontario K1P 5T1 Canada
Phone: (613) 688-5335
Fax: (613) 688-3082

United Nations
2 United Nations Plaza
New York, NY 10017

Canadian Tourism Commission
Suite 1400, Four Bentall Centre
1055 Dunsmuir Street, Box 49230
Vancouver, BC V7X 1L2 Canada
Phone: (604) 638-8300

Niagara Falls Tourism
5400 Robinson St.
Niagara Falls, Ontario L2G 2A6 Canada
Phone: (905) 356-6061
Fax: (905) 356-5567

Interesting Websites

http://www.niagarafalls.ca

http://www.cntower.ca

http://www.hrmacmillanspacecentre.com/

http://www.skylon.com/

Answer Key

Page 7
1. flag 2. Canada 3. six 4. sea to sea
5. Forests 6. people

Page 8
1. C 2. C

Page 9

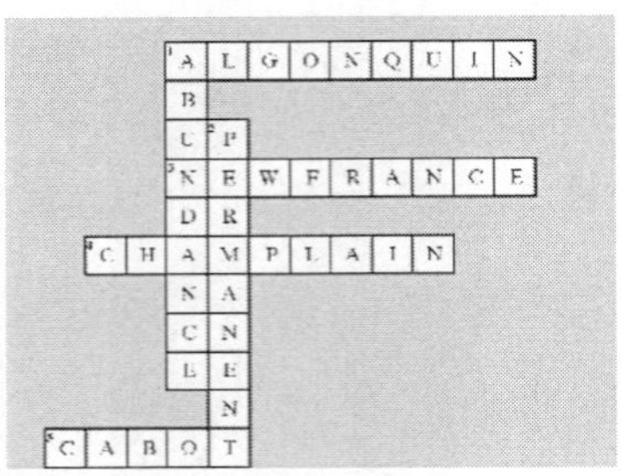

Page 10
5, 1, 4, 3, 2

Page 11
1. C 2. A 3. B 4. D 5. E 6. F

Page 12
Darcy Island - B, Jerome - C, War of 1812 - D,
Marie-Joseph Angelique - A,
Québec Separatism - E

Page 17
bunny hug - hoodie
fire hall - fire station
garburator - garbage disposal
parkade - parking garage
pencil crayon - colored pencil
runners - sneakers
serviette - napkin
tuque - knitted hat
washroom - bathroom

Page 21
1. 46 years
2. 1,200 hours

Page 22
Church - Basilique Cathédrale Notre Dame
Historical/Monument - Cartier-Brèbeuf National Historic Site, National Battlefields Park
Natural - Montmorency Falls

Page 25
Turret

Page 26
Yorkville

Page 29
St. Michael's Cathedral